Andrew Langley

Language consultant
Diana Bentley
University of Reading

Artist
Mike Atkinson

Let's Look At

Aircraft	Dinosaurs	Sharks
Bears	Farming	Ships and Boats
Big Cats	Horses	Sunshine
Bikes	Monster Machines	Tractors
Birds	Outer Space	Trains
Castles	Racing Cars	Trucks
Circuses	Rain	Volcanoes
Colours	The Seasons	Whales

Editor: Anna Girling

First published in 1990 by
Wayland (Publishers) Ltd
61 Western Road, Hove
East Sussex BN3 1JD, England

© Copyright 1990 Wayland (Publishers) Ltd

British Library Cataloguing in Publication Data
Langley, Andrew
    Racing cars.
    1. racing cars. Racing
    I. Title II. Atkinson, Michael
    796.7′2

ISBN 1-85210-832-0

Phototypeset by Kalligraphics Ltd, Horley, Surrey
Printed and bound by Casterman, S.A., Belgium

Words printed in **bold** are explained in the glossary

Contents

On and off the track 4
How a racing car works 6
The first racing cars 8
Smaller and faster 10
Racing cars today 12
At the circuit 14
In the pits 16
They're off! 18
Rally cars 20
Stock cars 22
Drag racing 24
The quest for speed 26
Racing cars of the future 28

Glossary 30
Books to read 31
Index 32

On and off the track

Racing cars are the fastest cars of all. They are built for speed. They have big, powerful engines and light bodies. They race against each other to see which is the fastest.

There are many different kinds of racing cars. **Grand Prix** cars are driven round special tracks called **circuits**. Rally cars are **saloon cars** which race along courses on ordinary roads. Stock cars bump over rough tracks.

How a racing car works

This is a modern racing car. It is very different from a family saloon car. There are no mudguards or windscreen. The huge engine is at the back. It drives the back wheels. These have big, wide tyres which grip the road well.

The car's engine is powered by petrol. The fuel tank is behind the driver's seat. It holds more than 180 litres of petrol.

The curved bar over the fuel tank is called a roll bar. It helps to protect the driver if the car turns over during a race.

The first racing cars

The very first motor race was held in France in 1894. The winning car was powered by a **steam engine**.

Early petrol car

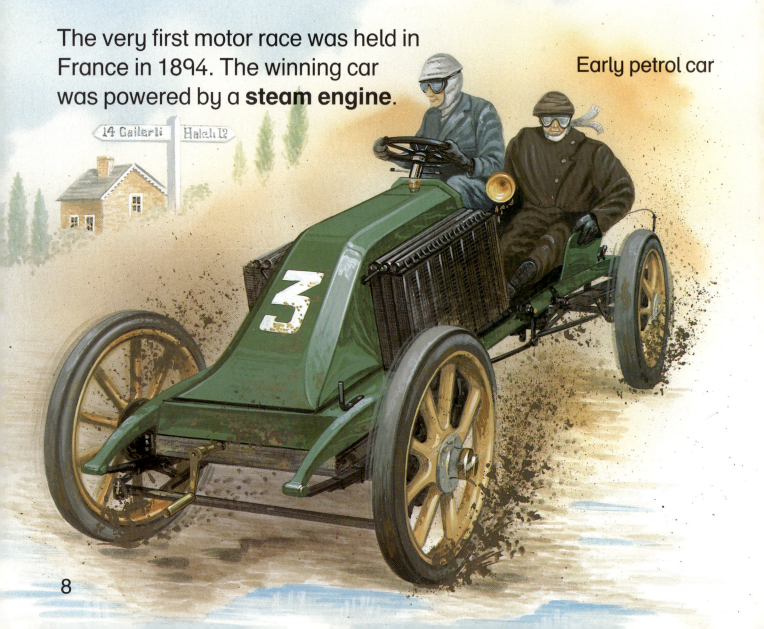

Cars with steam engines were very slow. Cars with petrol engines soon showed that they were much faster and more reliable. Motor racing quickly became a popular sport in Europe and America.

The early racing cars were difficult to drive. They had no springs so they were very uncomfortable. Their brakes were weak and their engines were very noisy. The driver sat in a hard seat.

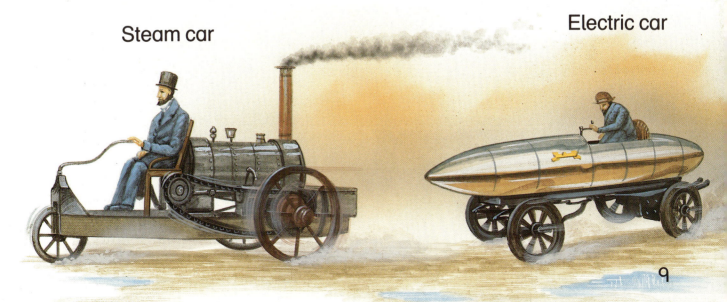

Steam car

Electric car

Smaller and faster

The most famous racing car in the 1920s was the Italian Bugatti. It could pick up speed very quickly. Bugattis won hundreds of races.

Bugatti (1920s)

Gradually racing cars became smaller and faster. Their brakes were safer. They had better **suspension** so they could go round sharp bends more easily.

By the 1950s, new cars had **streamlined** bodies. The British Vanwall was specially curved so that air could flow more easily over it. This meant it could travel faster.

Vanwall (1950s)

Ferrari (1950s)

Racing cars today

Grand Prix cars today have their bodies and **chassis** made in one piece. They are light and very strong.

Modern cars also have aerofoils at the front and back. These look like short aircraft wings. Air flowing over them helps to press the car downwards onto the track and prevents it from slipping.

The tyres of modern racing cars have also changed. When they warm up they become sticky, almost like chewing gum, and they grip the road more firmly.

This is an American racing car.

At the circuit

Cars are carried to the racing circuit in huge lorries called transporters. Each transporter has room for three cars and all their spare parts and tools. It is also used as a changing room and an office.

A team of skilled **mechanics** looks after the cars. They take them to the **paddock** near the race track. Here they make a careful check of each car, to make sure that it is ready for the race.

They're off!

The racing cars line up on the **starting grid**. Their roaring engines make a deafening noise. The drivers watch a set of lights. When the lights turn green, the race begins.

The cars race round the circuit. The drivers pull into the pits to refill their fuel tanks or have their cars repaired very quickly.

Most Grand Prix races last for many **laps**, and cover over 250 km. When the leading car crosses the finishing line, a black and white chequered flag is waved.

Rally cars

A rally is a race for saloon cars. It takes place on ordinary roads, over a specially set course. Each driver has a **navigator**, who reads a map of the course and tells him which route to take.

Most rallies last for several days. Some take place on twisting mountain roads. Others cross deserts or wind through narrow city streets. The longest rally of all is the East African Safari Rally in Kenya.

Stock cars

A stock car is an ordinary saloon car which has been made more powerful. It is also made as light as possible by removing any extra equipment such as lights, windows and wipers.

Stock car races can be held almost anywhere. Some take place on racing circuits and some on grass fields. The drivers try to knock their cars into their rivals' cars and push them off the track. There are plenty of accidents, but few people are badly injured.

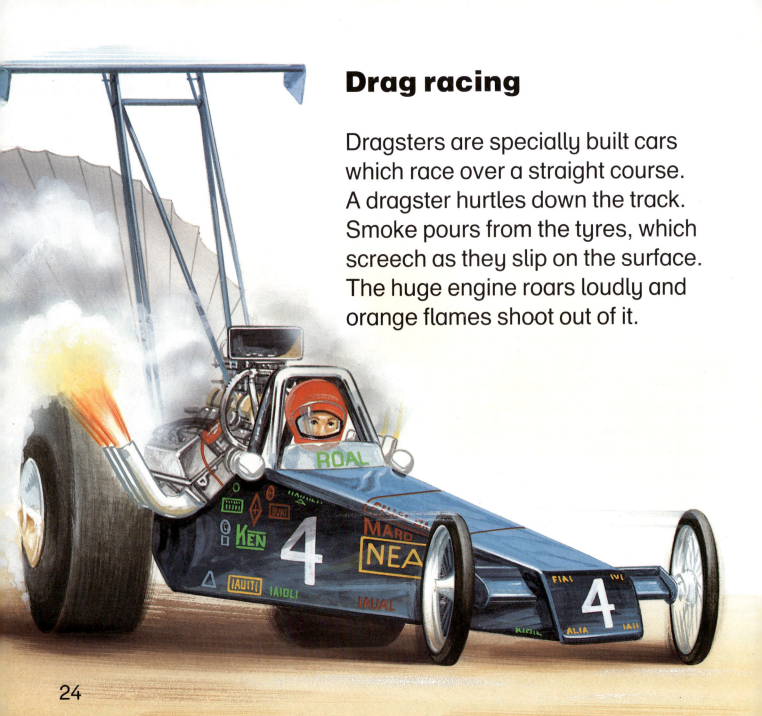

Drag racing

Dragsters are specially built cars which race over a straight course. A dragster hurtles down the track. Smoke pours from the tyres, which screech as they slip on the surface. The huge engine roars loudly and orange flames shoot out of it.

Dragsters cover the course in only a few seconds and reach speeds of more than 400 kph. In fact, they go so fast that ordinary brakes will not stop them quickly enough. Parachutes are used to help slow them down.

The quest for speed

Ever since cars were invented, people have wanted them to go faster. Here are some famous holders of the **land speed record**.

The first land speed record was set in 1898. An electric car, the *Never Content*, travelled at 63 kph.

The fastest car with a petrol engine was the *Bluebird*, driven by Donald Campbell. In 1964 it reached a speed of 690 kph.

Never Content

Thrust 2

The fastest of all land vehicles is Richard Noble's *Thrust 2*. In 1983 *Thrust 2*, powered by a **jet engine**, travelled at a speed of 1019 kph.

Bluebird

Index

A
America 9, 13

B
Bluebird 26, 27
Bugatti 10

C
Chequered flag 19
Circuit 4, 14–15, 19, 23

D
Dragsters 24–5

E
Engines 4, 7, 8, 9, 18, 24, 26–7, 29

F
Ferrari 11
France 8
Fuel tank 7, 19

G
Grand Prix 4, 12, 19

L
Land speed record 26

N
Never Content 26

P
Paddock 15
Petrol 7, 9, 26
Pits 16–17, 19

R
Rally cars 4, 20–21

S
Saloon cars 4, 7, 20, 22
Starting grid 18
Stock cars 4, 22–3
Suspension 11

T
Thrust 2 27
Transporters 15
Tyres 7, 13, 24

V
Vanwall 11
Visor 17